Reading Together

Beans on toast

Read it together

Just about every child likes beans on toast! Here's a chance for children to see where they come from in this enjoyable information book.

One of the most important ways of helping your child to read is by reading aloud and this is true of information books too. It's a good way of introducing children to a wide variety of different kinds of books.

This book shows how baked beans are produced. Children can use the cartoon-style pictures to predict the next stage in the process and to match their ideas to the words on the page.

With experience, help from the pictures and the repeated word pattern, children may be reading this book for themselves quite quickly. Don't worry if the words aren't always the same as those on the page.

If children are reading and get stuck on a word, you can help them to guess. Encourage them to look at the pictures and at the first letter of the word, or to read on and come back to it. It's a good idea to just give them the word if they're really stuck or tired.

Beans on ...

Look at the picture. Beans on ...

toast!

Look at the way it starts. "To" for Toby and ...

Sometimes you can help children to look more closely at the actual words and letters. See if they can find words they recognize, or letters from their name. Help them to write some of the words they know.

toast!

I know another book with beans in it.

Talk about books with them and discuss the stories and pictures. Compare other books with *Beans on toast.*

Jack and the Beanstalk?

The Hairy Toe!

We hope you enjoy reading this book together.

For Carol and Peter

First published 1998 by Walker Books Ltd
87 Vauxhall Walk, London SE11 5HJ

2 4 6 8 10 9 7 5 3 1

© 1998 Paul Dowling
Introductory and concluding notes © 1998 CLPE

Printed in Great Britain

ISBN 0-7445-4882-9

Beans on toast

Paul Dowling

WALKER BOOKS

AND SUBSIDIARIES

LONDON • BOSTON • SYDNEY

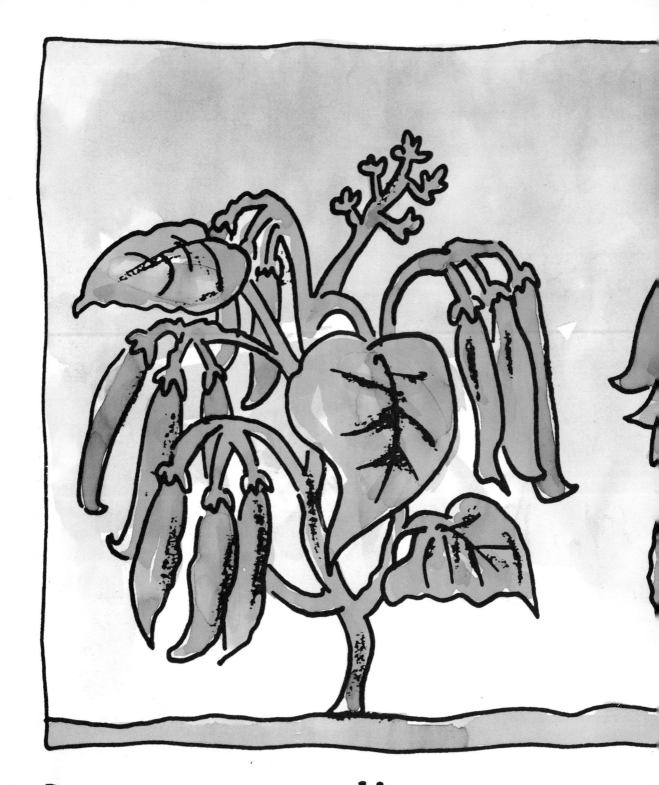

Beans on stalks

Beans on legs

Beans on racks

Beans on wheels

Beans on the road

Beans on cranes

Beans on the boil

Beans on tins

Beans on trucks

Beans on shelves

Beans on the counter

Beans on the way home

Beans on cooker

Beans on spoon

Beans on head

Beans on floor

Beans on toast

Read it again

Map the journey

This book shows, in an amusing way, how beans move from the field to the plate. With your help, children can map the journey in a simple diagram. Perhaps they can act it out, too.

Plan the day

Many everyday activities can be mapped out, such as cooking, painting and getting dressed. You could plan one out together.

First I put on my pants, then my socks...

What happens next?

You could talk together about what happens after the end of the story in the book. Your child can draw what happens to the bean tin.

Mum put the empty tin in the bin ...

and then the dustman took it to be recycled and made into a new tin.

And maybe we bought it again when we went shopping!

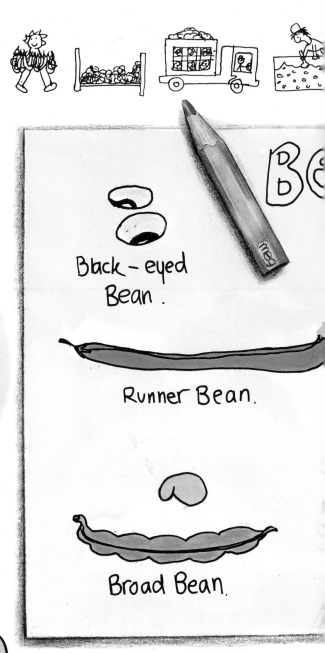

Black - eyed Bean.

Runner Bean.

Broad Bean.

Beans, beans, beans!

When shopping or cooking, you can look at different kinds of beans together — fresh and tinned. Children can talk about them, taste and draw them. They can describe them for you to write a label next to each picture.

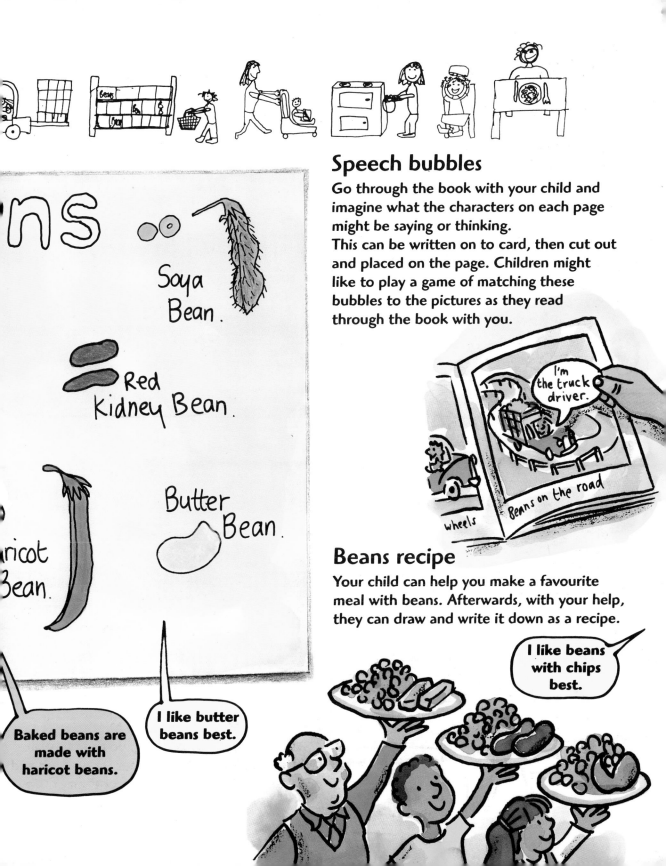

ns

Soya Bean.

Red Kidney Bean.

Butter Bean.

Haricot Bean.

Baked beans are made with haricot beans.

I like butter beans best.

Speech bubbles

Go through the book with your child and imagine what the characters on each page might be saying or thinking.

This can be written on to card, then cut out and placed on the page. Children might like to play a game of matching these bubbles to the pictures as they read through the book with you.

I'm the truck driver.

wheels

Beans on the road

Beans recipe

Your child can help you make a favourite meal with beans. Afterwards, with your help, they can draw and write it down as a recipe.

I like beans with chips best.

Reading Together

The *Reading Together* series is divided into four levels – starting with red, then on to yellow, blue and finally green. The six books in each level offer children varied experiences of reading. There are stories, poems, rhymes and songs, traditional tales and information books to choose from.

Accompanying the series is a Parents' Handbook, which looks at all the different ways children learn to read and explains how *your* help can really make a difference!